DASH Diet for Beginners

Easy and Delicious DASH Diet Recipes to Lose Weight and Lower Blood Pressure

Savannah Gibbs

Table of Contents

Chapter 1: Introduction to the DASH Diet

The DASH diet was developed from medical research, and the original intent of this eating program was to lower blood pressure. In fact, that's what DASH stands for: **D**ietary **A**pproaches to **S**top **H**ypertension. In addition to the benefit of lowering blood pressure, many people who follow the DASH diet lose weight because of the healthy foods the diet recommends.

A Brief History of the DASH Diet

In the mid-90s, large-scale studies were conducted at prestigious universities and medical centers to find new diet plans that could help hypertension patients lower blood pressure. These studies, combined with follow-up studies and research, led to the development of the DASH diet plan. Today, the DASH diet is recommended by several important organizations, including the American Heart Association and the National Heart, Lung, and Blood Institute. The recommendations in this diet are the basis for the U.S. Dietary Guidelines, and most doctors prescribe the DASH plan to patients who are battling high blood pressure. The DASH diet takes a scientific approach to good health, not by counting calories or measuring grams of fat, but by a holistic approach of choosing the foods that are most likely to keep a body healthy.

DASH Diet: The Principles

The DASH diet focuses on long-term healthy eating habits. The diet doesn't force you to starve or battle constant cravings.

Instead, it focuses on understanding food groups, controlling portion sizes, and making sure you get the optimal levels of potassium, calcium, magnesium, fiber, and protein.

The diet focuses certain food groups for specific reasons: Fruits and vegetables give you the magnesium and potassium your body needs, and low-fat dairy products provide calcium. Every food you eat should have a purpose, and that's the most important principle of the DASH diet: eat well so you feel well. Here are some additional points to remember when you're following the DASH principles:

• Reduce your sodium intake. The diet recommends less than 2,300 mg of sodium per day. The National Heart, Lung and Blood Institute recommends lowering the sodium intake even further—to 1,500 mg—for people with high blood pressure, people with diabetes or chronic kidney disease, African Americans, and people aged 51 and over.

• Eat fruits, vegetables, and low-fat dairy products
• Focus on high-fiber foods
• Eat more healthy fats, which are good for your heart, instead of saturated fats
• Achieve and maintain a healthy body weight
• Eat a lot of potassium and magnesium
• Stay hydrated by drinking plenty of plain water
• Avoid smoking

The DASH diet is more than just a diet—it's a lifestyle.

DASH Diet: Health Benefits

There are many health benefits associated with the DASH diet. Weight loss is one of the most important benefits, and it's a leading reason why people adopt the diet. The diet also brings down blood pressure, which can go hand-in-hand with weight loss and is an important medical reason why people follow this eating plan. In addition to improving blood pressure, the

DASH diet has been praised for lowering the risk and reducing the symptoms of other chronic diseases, like heart disease, kidney disease, and diabetes. You'll have a lot more energy on this eating plan because your blood sugar will be stable and your metabolism will speed up. The fruits and veggies you fill up on will provide you with a lot of cancer-fighting and immune-boosting antioxidants, and many people report looking and feeling younger, as well.

DASH Diet for Lowering Blood Pressure

Elevated blood pressure can cause a long list of health problems. With high blood pressure, your heart is working too hard to keep up with the normal functions of your body, and this leads to a higher risk of a heart attack or stroke. A major culprit of elevated blood pressure is salt, or sodium, and that's a target of the DASH diet: to eliminate the excess sodium in your body and replace it with nutrients that are far more beneficial. Foods rich in potassium and magnesium have been found to help your body reduce blood pressure naturally. According to scientific studies, the DASH eating plan is just as effective as many blood pressure medications. So, instead of popping pills, you can simply follow the DASH diet to reduce your blood pressure and live a healthier life.

DASH Diet for Weight Loss

Early versions of the DASH diet focused solely on blood pressure and didn't aim to help people lose weight. When patients on this eating plan began to lose weight naturally, however, people began to realize what a valuable weight loss tool it was. This diet is a great way to lose weight because it incorporates fresh, whole foods and reduces packaged, processed foods that are filled with empty calories. Not only will you lose weight, you'll also have a better chance of keeping it off. DASH goes beyond the calorie counting and helps you establish sound eating habits that improve your chances for maintaining healthy weight.

What to Eat on the DASH Diet

Healthy, high-fiber grains that are low in sugar are a great way to start on the DASH diet. These include whole grain cereals and breads, brown rice, and whole wheat pasta. Next, you should aim for four or five servings of fruits and vegetables every day. Recommended vegetables include lettuce, cabbage, celery, carrots, spinach, squash, broccoli, cucumbers, tomatoes, and mushrooms. Recommended fruits include blackberries, blueberries, strawberries, apples, pears, bananas, avocados, citrus fruits, melons, and mangos.

You can have milk, yogurt, and cheese too, just be sure to watch for added salt and sugar in these products. Nuts and legumes are also big parts of the DASH diet. Get your protein from beans, eggs, and lean meats. In addition, the DASH diet encourages fish, such as salmon, tilapia, and mackerel.

What to Avoid on the DASH Diet

It's essential to stay away from salt and trans fats when you're following the DASH diet. Use olive oil instead of butter, and stick to healthy food preparations like steaming and grilling. Keep sauces to a minimum, and while snacking is encouraged, choose healthy snacks instead of processed foods that are high in calories and added sodium.

Transitioning to the DASH Diet

Changing your eating habits needs to be done gradually. Here are a few suggestions to help you make an easy transition to the DASH diet:

- Keep a journal and track your eating habits. What do you eat for breakfast, lunch, and dinner? How often do you eat in between meals, and what are you snacking on? From your journal, you can figure out where you need to make changes. For example, add a cup or two of vegetables and fruits to help reduce too many servings of meat. Limit your sodium and sugar by reading the nutrition facts labels on food packages.
- When shopping, choose "low-fat," "non-fat," "no sugar added," "no cholesterol," and other healthier versions of products. For grain servings, choose whole grains, such as whole wheat bread and whole grain cereals.
- If you love butter or margarine, decrease the amount you use by half and switch to no-cholesterol and low-sodium versions. You can use spices as a substitute for salt. Experiment with different herbs if you're not sure how they taste. Some examples of spices you can try are rosemary, basil, nutmeg, parsley, sage, and thyme.

This book will make following the DASH diet much easier for you, and the 67 delicious recipes included will help you make dietary changes, lower your blood pressure, and lose weight.

Chapter 2: DASH Diet Breakfast Recipes

These breakfast recipes follow the DASH diet plan for lowering your blood pressure. The meals are full of fruits, vegetables, whole grains, and healthy dairy products. Start the day off with one of these scrumptious meals and you'll reduce your risk for cardiovascular problems and weight gain.

Multigrain Hot Cereal

Yield: 8 servings
Ingredients:
½ cup pearl barley
½ cup red wheat berries
½ cup brown rice
¼ cup steel cut oats
3 tablespoons quinoa
¼ teaspoon kosher salt

1½ quarts water

Directions:

1. Add all ingredients to a saucepan, stir to mix and bring to a boil.

2. Reduce the heat to low and allow to simmer for 45 minutes giving it an occasional stir.

3. The cereal can be refrigerated and reheated for quick breakfasts or snacks throughout the week.

Nutritional Information (Per Serving)
Calories: 118
Fat: 1.0 g
Sat Fat: 0 g
Carbohydrates: 23.6 g
Fiber: 4.3 g
Sugar: 0.6 g
Protein: 4.0 g
Sodium: 74.6 mg

Buckwheat Dates Granola

Yield: 12 servings

Ingredients:

2 cups oats
1 cup buckwheat groats
1 cup pumpkin seeds
1 cup sunflower seeds
1½ cups dates, pitted and chopped
1 cup apple puree
1/3 cup coconut oil
1 teaspoon fresh ginger, grated finely
¼ cup raw cacao powder

Directions:

1. Preheat the oven to 355 degrees F. Grease a large baking dish.

2. In a large bowl, add oats, buckwheat, and seeds, and mix well.

3. In a pan, mix together dates, apple puree, and coconut oil over medium-low heat. Simmer, stirring continuously for about 5 minutes until dates become soft.

4. Stir in ginger, immediately remove from heat, and set aside to cool slightly.

5. In a blender, add date mixture and cacao powder, and pulse until a smooth mixture forms.

6. Add the date mixture to the bowl with oat mixture, and stir to combine well.

7. Transfer the mixture to a baking dish. Bake for 15 minutes. Mix granola with a spatula.

8. Bake for 20–25 minutes until granola is crispy.

9. This granola can be preserved in an airtight container.

Nutritional Information (Per Serving)
Calories: 281

Fat: 13.3 g
Sat Fat: 5.5 g
Carbohydrates: 38.1 g
Fiber: 5.7 g
Sugar: 15.7 g
Protein: 7.6 g
Sodium: 5 mg

Oat & Nut Granola

Yield: 22 servings

Ingredients:

¼ cup applesauce

¼ cup canola oil

1½ teaspoons vanilla extract

6 cups old-fashioned rolled oats

2 cups bran flakes

1 cup almonds, slivered

¾ cup walnuts, chopped

½ cup unsweetened coconut, shredded

1 cup raisins

Directions:

1. Preheat oven to 325 degrees F. Lightly grease a baking sheet.

2. In a small pan over low heat, add applesauce, oil, and vanilla extract.

3. Cook for about 5 minutes, stirring occasionally.

4. Add remaining ingredients except for raisins and stir gently to combine.

5. Transfer the mixture onto prepared baking sheet.

6. Bake for about 25 minutes or until golden brown, stirring occasionally.

7. Remove from oven and set aside to cool.

8. Add raisins and stir to combine.

9. Granola may be preserved in airtight container.

Nutritional Information (Per Serving)

Calories: 197

Fat: 9.5 g

Sat Fat: 1.3 g

Carbohydrates: 25 g

Fiber: 4.1 g

Sugar: 5.9 g

Protein: 5.3 g
Sodium: 28 mg

Wheat Bagel with Apple

Yield: 2 servings

Ingredients:

1 whole wheat, whole grain bagel

1 apple, sliced

2 tablespoons peanut butter, reduced salt

Directions:

1. Toast your bagel, unless you prefer it untoasted, in which case you only need to slice it.

2. Spread the peanut butter on each side of the bagel (make sure you use a brand that has no added salt) and layer the apple slices on top of the peanut butter.

Nutritional Information (Per Serving)

Calories: 251

Fat: 8.9 g

Sat Fat: 1.3 g

Carbohydrates: 41.5 g

Fiber: 7.5 g

Sugar: 11.5 g

Protein: 9.5 g

Sodium: 268 mg

Eggs with Cheese

Yield: 1 serving

Ingredients:

1 egg

1 egg white

2 tablespoons fat-free milk

½ ounce grated cheddar cheese, reduced fat

1 green onion, chopped

¼ cup tomato, chopped

1 slice whole wheat bread

Directions:

1. Mix the egg and egg whites in a bowl and add the milk.

2. Scramble the mixture in a non-stick frying pan until the eggs cook.

3. Meanwhile, toast the bread.

4. Spoon the scrambled egg mixture onto the toasted bread and top with the cheese until it melts.

5. Add the onion and the tomato.

Nutritional Information (Per Serving)

Calories: 251

Fat: 11.0 g

Sat Fat: 4.7 g

Carbohydrates: 22.3 g

Fiber: 3.0 g

Sugar: 3.3 g

Protein: 16.9 g

Sodium: 337 mg

Carrot Bread

Yield: 8 servings

Ingredients:

2 cups almond flour

1 teaspoon baking powder

1 tablespoon cumin seeds

½ teaspoon salt

3 large eggs

2 tablespoons olive oil

1 tablespoon apple cider vinegar

3 cups carrots, peeled and grated

½ teaspoon fresh ginger, peeled and grated finely

¼ cup raisins

Directions:

1. Preheat the oven to 350 degrees F.

2. Line a loaf pan with parchment paper.

3. In a large bowl, add almond flour, baking powder, cumin seeds, and salt and mix well.

4. In another bowl, add the eggs, olive oil, and vinegar, and beat until well combined.

5. Add egg mixture to the flour mixture, and mix until well combined.

6. Gently fold in carrot, ginger, and raisins.

7. Place the mixture into the prepared loaf pan.

8. Bake for about 1 hour until a toothpick inserted in the center comes out clean.

Nutritional Information (Per Serving)

Calories: 253

Fat: 19.4 g

Sat Fat: 2.1 g

Carbohydrates: 14.8 g

Fiber: 4.6 g

Sugar: 6.0 g

Protein: 9.1 g
Sodium: 268 mg

Mushroom Muffins

Yield: 6 servings

Ingredients:

1 teaspoon olive oil
1½ cups fresh mushrooms, chopped
1 scallion, chopped
1 teaspoon garlic, minced
1 teaspoon fresh rosemary, minced
Freshly ground black pepper to taste
1 (12.3-ounce) package lite, firm, silken tofu, drained
¼ cup unsweetened soy milk
2 tablespoons nutritional yeast
1 tablespoon arrowroot starch
1 teaspoon unsalted butter, softened
¼ teaspoon ground turmeric

Directions:

1. Preheat oven to 375 degrees F. Grease a 12-cup muffin pan.

2. In a nonstick skillet, heat oil on medium heat.

3. Add scallion and garlic and sauté for about 1 minute.

4. Add mushrooms and sauté for about 5-7 minutes.

5. Stir in rosemary and black pepper and remove from the heat.

6. Keep aside to cool slightly.

7. In a food processor, add tofu and remaining ingredients and pulse until smooth.

8. Transfer tofu mixture into a large bowl.

9. Fold in mushroom mixture.

10. Spoon mixture evenly into prepared muffin cups.

11. Bake for about 20-22 minutes or until a toothpick inserted in center comes out clean.

12. Remove muffin pan from oven and place on wire rack to cool for about 10 minutes.

13. Carefully, invert muffins onto wire rack and serve warm.

Nutritional Information (Per Serving)
Calories: 88
Fat: 4.2 g
Sat Fat: 1 g
Carbohydrates: 7.3 g
Fiber: 1.4 g
Sugar: 1.9 g
Protein: 7.2 g
Sodium: 21 mg

Oat Smoothie

Yield: 4 servings

Ingredients:

2/3 cups rolled oats

2 oranges, peeled, seeded, and sectioned

2 large bananas, peeled and sliced

2 cups unsweetened almond milk

1 cup ice cubes, crushed

Directions:

1. In a high-speed blender, add rolled oats and pulse until finely chopped.

2. Add remaining ingredients and pulse until smooth.

3. Transfer into 4 serving glasses and serve immediately.

Nutritional Information (Per Serving)

Calories: 175

Fat: 3 g

Sat Fat: 0.4 g

Carbohydrates: 36.6 g

Fiber: 5.9 g

Sugar: 17.1 g

Protein: 3.9 g

Sodium: 93 mg

Berry Bowl

Yield: 2 servings

Ingredients:

2 cups frozen blueberries

1/3 cup unsweetened almond milk

¼ cup fat-free plain Greek yogurt

2 tablespoons unsweetened whey protein powder

¼ cup fresh blueberries

Directions:

1. In a blender, add blueberries and pulse for about 1 minute.

2. Add almond milk, yogurt, and protein powder and pulse until desired consistency.

3. Transfer the mixture into 2 serving bowls, dividing evenly.

4. Serve topped with fresh blueberries.

Nutritional Information (Per Serving)

Calories: 160

Fat: 1.8 g

Sat Fat: 0.2 g

Carbohydrates: 23.5 g

Fiber: 3.7 g

Sugar: 16.1 g

Protein: 15.3 g

Sodium: 70 mg

French Toasts Casserole

Yield: 2 servings
Ingredients:
2 whole-wheat bread slices, cubed
2 teaspoons unsalted margarine, softened
1 cup egg whites, slightly beaten
2 tablespoons applesauce
2 tablespoons almonds, chopped

Directions:
1. In a microwave safe bowl, mix the cubed bread and margarine.
2. Top with egg whites evenly and drizzle with applesauce.
3. Microwave on high for about 1 minute.
4. Remove from microwave and push away the edges of egg whites with a spoon.
5. Microwave for about 1 minute more.
6. Remove from microwave and divide into 2 portions.
7. Serve warm, topped with almonds.

Nutritional Information (Per Serving)
Calories: 207
Fat: 7.9 g
Sat Fat: 1.1 g
Carbohydrates: 15.5 g
Fiber: 2.8 g
Sugar: 4.2 g
Protein: 18.2 g
Sodium: 299 mg

Veggie Scramble

Yield: 4 servings

Ingredients:

½ cup chickpea flour

2 tablespoons nutritional yeast

2 teaspoons mustard

¼ teaspoon paprika

¼ teaspoon ground turmeric

1/8 teaspoon ground cumin

Freshly ground black pepper to taste

1/3 cup water

1½ cups cooked chickpeas

2 tablespoons fresh parsley, chopped

1 garlic clove, minced

1 tablespoon olive oil

½ bell pepper, seeded and chopped

½ onion, chopped

1 cup cherry tomatoes, halved

Directions:

1. In food processor, add chickpea flour, nutritional yeast, mustard, spices, and black pepper and pulse until well combined.

2. With motor slowly running, add water and mix until smooth mixture forms.

3. Add chickpeas and pulse until finely chopped.

4. Add parsley and garlic and mix well.

5. In a large skillet, heat oil on medium-high heat.

6. Add bell pepper and onion and sauté for about 5-6 minutes.

7. Add chickpea mixture and cook, stirring continuously for about 3-4 minutes.

8. Add tomatoes and reduce heat to medium.

9. Cook for about 10 minutes, turning tomatoes at the five-minute mark.

Nutritional Information (Per Serving)
Calories: 235
Fat: 7 g
Sat Fat: 0.6 g
Carbohydrates: 34 g
Fiber: 10.2 g
Sugar: 7.3 g
Protein: 12 g
Sodium: 17 mg

Quinoa Porridge

Yield: 4 servings

Ingredients:

2 cups unsweetened soy milk

1 cup uncooked quinoa, rinsed

¼ teaspoon vanilla extract

Pinch of ground cinnamon

1 date, pitted and chopped very finely

1 cup banana, peeled and sliced

Directions:

1. In a pan, combine milk, quinoa, vanilla, and cinnamon on low heat.

2. Cook, stirring occasionally for about 15-20 minutes.

3. Remove from heat and stir in chopped date.

4. Top with banana slices and serve.

Nutritional Information (Per Serving)

Calories: 263

Fat: 4.9 g

Sat Fat: 0.6 g

Carbohydrates: 45.2 g

Fiber: 4.9 g

Sugar: 10.8 g

Protein: 10.5 g

Sodium: 65 mg

Chicken Quiche

Yield: 8 servings

Ingredients:

1 teaspoon olive oil

½ cup onion, sliced

2 garlic cloves, minced

3 cups small broccoli florets

2 cups cooked chicken, chopped

2 large eggs

4 large egg whites

1¼ cups fat-free milk

1 cup fat-free Cheddar cheese, shredded

Freshly ground black pepper to taste

1 tablespoon low-fat Parmesan cheese, shredded

Directions:

1. Preheat oven to 350 degrees F. Grease a 9-inch pie plate.

2. In a skillet, heat oil on medium heat.

3. Add onion and garlic and sauté for about 2-3 minutes.

4. Add broccoli and chicken and sauté for about 1-2 minutes.

5. Transfer mixture to prepared pie dish.

6. In a bowl, add eggs, egg whites, milk, cheddar cheese, salt, and black pepper and beat until well-combined.

7. Pour egg mixture over chicken mixture and top with Parmesan cheese.

8. Bake for about 40 minutes or until top is golden brown.

9. Remove from oven. Cut into 8 equal-sized wedges and serve.

Nutritional Information (Per Serving)

Calories: 190

Fat: 7.9 g

Sat Fat: 3.8 g

Carbohydrates: 7.7 g
Fiber: 1 g
Sugar: 5.3 g
Protein: 2.1 g
Sodium: 210 mg

Tapioca Pancakes

Yield: 6 servings

Ingredients:

½ cup tapioca flour
½ cup almond flour
½ teaspoon red chili powder
¼ teaspoon salt
Black pepper to taste
1 cup coconut milk
½ red onion, chopped
¼ teaspoon fresh ginger, minced
1 serrano pepper, seeded and minced
½ cup fresh parsley leaves, chopped
2 tablespoons olive oil

Directions:

1. In a large bowl, mix together flours and spices. Add the coconut milk, and mix until well combined.

2. Fold in the onion, ginger, serrano pepper, and cilantro.

3. Lightly grease a large nonstick skillet with oil, and heat over medium heat.

4. Add about ¼ cup of mixture, and tilt the pan to spread it evenly in the skillet. Cook for about 3–4 minutes for both sides.

5. Repeat with the remaining mixture.

6. Serve with your desired topping.

Nutritional Information (Per Serving)
Calories: 146
Fat: 10.1 g
Sat Fat: 1.8 g
Carbohydrates: 13.1 g
Fiber: 1.4 g
Sugar: 1.4 g
Protein: 2.4 g

Sodium: 107 mg

Chicken Breakfast Burrito

Yield: 2 servings

Ingredients:

4 ounces cooked skinless chicken

1 whole wheat tortilla

1 cup fresh spinach

1 pear, sliced

2 tablespoons Italian salad dressing

Directions:

1. Slice the chicken into small bite-sized pieces and arrange them on the tortilla.

2. Cover the meat with spinach and arrange the pear slices on top.

3. Drizzle with Italian salad dressing.

4. Wrap the tortilla around all the ingredients until it's a snug burrito.

Nutritional Information (Per Serving)

Calories: 246

Fat: 10.3 g

Sat Fat: 1.9 g

Carbohydrates: 23.6 g

Fiber: 4.0 g

Sugar: 7.9 g

Protein: 15.6 g

Sodium: 298 mg

Chapter 3: DASH Diet Lunch Recipes

When you're looking for DASH diet lunch recipes, you're looking for food that's healthy but filling. There are many fruits, vegetables, whole grains, and lean proteins that combine to make fresh, tasty, and healthful meals that you can eat at home or at work. These recipes will give you a bolt of energy in the middle of the day and feed your body with the vitamins, nutrients, and ingredients that it really needs and craves.

Citrus Shrimp Salad

Yield: 4 servings

Ingredients:

½ pound cooked small salad shrimp, peeled and rinsed

¼ cup freshly squeezed orange juice

1 tablespoon balsamic vinegar

6 cups spinach and lettuce mix

1 cucumber, chopped

2 oranges, peeled and chopped

Directions:

1. Combine the shrimp with the orange juice, vinegar and cucumber and toss.

2. Chill the mixture in the refrigerator for at least 30 minutes.

3. Place the mixture on top of the lettuce and spinach and sprinkle with orange segments.

Nutritional Information (Per Serving)

Calories: 125

Fat: 0.8 g

Sat Fat: 0.2 g

Carbohydrates: 15.6 g

Fiber: 3.8 g

Sugar: 8.2 g

Protein: 14.4 g

Sodium: 164 mg

Fruity Wheat Berry Salad

Yield: 4 servings
Ingredients:
For Salad:
2 cups water
1 cup wheat berries
1 cup mango, peeled, pitted, and cubed
1 cup pineapple, chopped
1 red bell pepper, seeded and chopped
2 scallions, chopped
½ cup fresh mint leaves, chopped
½ cup cranberries
½ cup walnuts, toasted and chopped
For Dressing:
1 tablespoon fresh ginger, minced
½ cup plain 2% Greek yogurt
3 tablespoons honey
½ teaspoon balsamic vinegar
¼ teaspoon salt
Black pepper to taste

Directions:
1. In a pan, add water and wheat berries, and bring to a boil. Cover and simmer for about 35 minutes.

2. Remove from heat, and set aside to cool completely.

3. In a large bowl, add wheat berries and remaining ingredients and mix.

4. In a small bowl, add dressing ingredients, and beat well.

5. Place dressing over salad mixture, and toss to coat well. Serve immediately.

Nutritional Information (Per Serving)
Calories: 379
Fat: 11.5 g

Sat Fat: 1.3 g
Carbohydrates: 66.5 g
Fiber: 10.2 g
Sugar: 26.3 g
Protein: 22.8 g
Sodium: 173 mg

Cabbage and Broccoli Salad

Yield: 4 servings
Ingredients:
For Dressing:
1 tablespoon shallot, minced
1/3 cup of olive oil
2 tablespoons fresh lemon juice
3 drops liquid stevia
Freshly ground black pepper to taste

For Salad:
1¼ cup broccoli florets, chopped
1¼ cups cabbage, shredded
6 cups romaine lettuce, chopped

Directions:
1. In a bowl, add all dressing ingredients and beat until well combined. Keep aside.
2. In another large bowl, mix all salad ingredients together.
3. Add dressing and toss gently to coat well.
4. Serve immediately.

Nutritional Information (Per Serving)
Calories: 174
Fat: 17.1 g
Sat Fat: 2.5 g
Carbohydrates: 6.2 g
Fiber: 1.9 g
Sugar: 2.2 g
Protein: 1.6 g
Sodium: 20 mg

Pear and Walnut Salad

Yield: 4 servings

Ingredients:

6 cups of mixed lettuces and greens

3 pears, thinly sliced

¼ cup toasted walnuts, chopped

1 fennel bulb, thinly sliced

2 tablespoons grated pecorino cheese

3 tablespoons extra virgin olive oil

3 tablespoons balsamic vinegar

Ground black pepper

Directions:

1. Wash the lettuces and place in a large bowl.

2. Spread the fennel and the pear over the lettuces and top with the cheese, oil, vinegar, and pepper.

3. Finish with the chopped walnuts.

Nutritional Information (Per Serving)

Calories: 245

Fat: 16.5 g

Sat Fat: 1.9 g

Carbohydrates: 24.9 g

Fiber: 6.3 g

Sugar: 11.2 g

Protein: 3.5 g

Sodium: 41.8 mg

Vegetable Sandwich

Yield: 4 servings

Ingredients:

1 avocado, peeled, pitted, and chopped

1 large tomato, sliced

½ cup red onion, sliced thinly

8 romaine lettuce leaves, chopped

8 whole wheat bread slices, toasted

¼ cup Dijon mustard

Directions:

1. In a large bowl, mix avocado, tomato, onion, and lettuce.

2. Evenly divide and spread Dijon mustard on each slice.

3. Evenly divide and place avocado mixture over 4 slices.

4. Cover with remaining slices.

5. With a knife, carefully cut sandwiches diagonally and serve.

Nutritional Information (Per Serving)

Calories: 267

Fat: 12.4 g

Sat Fat: 2.5 g

Carbohydrates: 31.7 g

Fiber: 31.7 g

Sugar: 5.4 g

Protein: 9.5 g

Sodium: 440 mg

Turkey Lettuce Wraps

Yield: 4 servings
Ingredients:
1 tablespoon olive oil
1 cup onion, chopped
¾ pound lean ground turkey
1 cup fresh mushrooms, chopped
½ tablespoon fresh ginger, minced
1 tablespoon soy sauce
½ tablespoon cayenne pepper
½ tablespoon ground cumin
8 large romaine lettuce leaves
2 tablespoons fresh cilantro leaves, chopped

Directions:
1. In a skillet, heat oil on medium heat.
2. Add onion and sauté for about 4-5 minutes.
3. Add turkey and cook for about 6-8 minutes, stirring occasionally.
4. Add mushroom, ginger, tamari, cayenne pepper, and cumin and cook for about 5-7 minutes.
5. Remove from heat and set aside.
6. Arrange lettuce leaves onto serving plates.
7. Place turkey mixture over each lettuce leaf evenly.
8. Top with cilantro and serve.

Nutritional Information (Per Serving)
Calories: 174
Fat: 9.6 g
Sat Fat: 2.4 g
Carbohydrates: 4.8 g
Fiber: 1.2 g
Sugar: 0.4 g
Protein: 18.1 g
Sodium: 317 mg

Bean Burgers

Yield: 6 servings

Ingredients:

½ cup walnuts

1 carrot, peeled and chopped

1 celery stalk, chopped

4 scallions, chopped

5 garlic cloves, chopped

2¼ cups cooked black beans

2½ cups sweet potato, peeled and grated

½ teaspoon red pepper flakes, crushed

Freshly ground black pepper to taste

10 cups fresh baby spinach

½ cup fresh pomegranate seeds

Directions:

1. Preheat the oven to 400 degrees F. Line a baking sheet with parchment paper.

2. Add walnuts to food processor, until finely ground.

3. Add carrot, celery, scallion, and garlic and pulse until finely chopped.

4. Transfer vegetable mixture to large bowl.

5. In same food processor, add beans and pulse until chopped.

6. Add 1½ cups sweet potato and pulse until chunky mixture forms.

7. Transfer bean mixture into bowl with vegetable mixture.

8. Stir in remaining sweet potato and spices and mix until well combined.

9. Make 8 patties from mixture.

10. Arrange patties on prepared baking sheet in a single layer.

11. Bake for about 25 minutes.

12. Divide spinach and pomegranate seeds evenly into 8 servings. Place each serving on a plate.

13. Top each plate with 1 burger and serve.

Nutritional Information (Per Serving)
Calories: 326
Fat: 5.9 g
Sat Fat: 0.5 g
Carbohydrates: 55.1 g
Fiber: 13 g
Sugar: 9.1 g
Protein: 16.6 g
Sodium: 64 mg

Broccoli with Apple

Yield: 4 servings

Ingredients:

1 tablespoon olive oil

2 garlic cloves, minced

2 cups small broccoli florets

½ cup red onion, chopped

¼ cup celery stalk, chopped

¼ cup low-sodium vegetable broth

2 apples, cored and sliced

Directions:

1. In a large skillet, heat oil on medium-high heat.
2. Add garlic and sauté for about 1 minute.
3. Add broccoli and stir fry for about 4-5 minutes.
4. Add celery and onion and stir fry for about 4-5 minutes.
5. Stir in broth and cook for about 2-3 minutes.
6. Add apple slices and cook for about 2-3 minutes.
7. Serve hot.

Nutritional Information (Per Serving)

Calories: 105

Fat: 3.7 g

Sat Fat: 0.5 g

Carbohydrates: 18.6 g

Fiber: 3.9 g

Sugar: 12.7 g

Protein: 1.1 g

Sodium: 56 mg

Green Beans and Tomato Combo

Yield: 6 servings

Ingredients:

2 teaspoons olive oil

¼ teaspoon fresh lemon peel, finely grated

Pinch of freshly ground white pepper

3 cups grape tomatoes

2 pounds fresh green beans, trimmed

1 tablespoon fresh parsley, chopped

Directions:

1. Preheat the oven to 350 degrees F.

2. In large bowl, mix lemon peel, oil, and white pepper.

3. Add cherry tomatoes and toss until well-coated.

4. Transfer tomato mixture to a roasting pan.

5. Roast for about 35-40 minutes, stirring once in half-way through.

6. Meanwhile, place steamer basket in a pan of boiling water.

7. Place green beans in steamer basket. Cover and steam for about 7-8 minutes. Drain well.

8. Divide green beans and tomatoes and place on serving plates.

9. Sprinkle with parsley and serve hot.

Nutritional Information (Per Serving)

Calories: 77

Fat: 1.9 g

Sat Fat: 0.3 g

Carbohydrates: 14.4 g

Fiber: 6.3 g

Sugar: 4.5 g

Protein: 3.6 g

Sodium: 17 mg

Southwestern Vegetable Tacos

Yield: 4 servings
Ingredients:
1 tablespoon olive oil
1 medium red onion, chopped
1 cup yellow summer squash, diced
1 cup green zucchini, diced
3 large garlic cloves, minced
4 medium tomatoes, seeded and chopped
1 jalapeno chili, seeded and chopped
1 cup frozen corn
1 cup canned black beans, rinsed and drained
½ cup cilantro, chopped
8 corn tortillas
½ cup salsa

Directions:
1. Heat the oil over medium heat in a large saucepan. Cook the onion until soft then add the squash and zucchini and cook until tender.

2. Next, add beans, corn, tomatoes, garlic, and jalapeños and cook until soft, about 5 minutes. Add the cilantro and remove the pot from heat.

3. Heat a dry frying pan over medium heat and warm tortillas on each side.

4. Place two tortillas on each plate and fill each tortilla equally with the vegetable mixture and top with salsa.

5. Serve and enjoy immediately.

Nutritional Information (Per Serving)
Calories: 303
Fat: 6.0 g
Sat Fat: 0.9 g
Carbohydrates: 56.8 g

Fiber: 11.6 g
Sugar: 3.5 g
Protein: 10.7 g
Sodium: 181 mg

Sautéed Mixed Mushrooms

Yield: 3 servings
Ingredients:
3 tablespoons extra virgin olive oil
3 portobello mushrooms, sliced
6 ounces shiitake mushrooms, stemmed and sliced
8 ounces button mushrooms
1 tablespoon fresh ginger, minced
5 garlic cloves, minced
1 dried red chili, crushed
2 teaspoons coconut aminos
1 teaspoon sesame oil

Directions:
1. In a skillet, heat 1 tablespoon of olive oil over medium heat.

2. Add portobello mushrooms, and cook for 4–5 minutes, stirring occasionally. Transfer the mushrooms into a large bowl.

3. In the same skillet, heat 1 tablespoon of olive oil on medium heat. Add shiitake and button mushrooms, and cook for 5–7 minutes.

4. Transfer the mushrooms into the large bowl with portobello mushrooms.

5. In the same skillet, heat remaining oil over medium heat. Add ginger, garlic, and red chili, and sauté for 1 minute.

6. Add the mushroom mixture, coconut aminos, and sesame oil, and stir until well combined. Cook for 1–2 minutes.

7. Serve hot.

Nutritional Information (Per Serving)
Calories: 211
Fat: 15.6 g

Sat Fat: 2.2 g
Carbohydrates: 15.8 g
Fiber: 3.4 g
Sugar: 5.6 g
Protein: 4.2 g
Sodium: 100 mg

Pasta Primavera

Yield: 4 servings

Ingredients:

12 ounces whole wheat pasta

1 garlic clove, chopped

1 red bell pepper, chopped

1 green bell pepper, chopped

1 yellow bell pepper, chopped

1 cucumber, chopped

1 red onion, chopped

1 can diced tomatoes, no salt added

2 tablespoons extra virgin olive oil

1 tablespoon lemon juice

½ teaspoon basil

½ teaspoon oregano

½ teaspoon rosemary

½ teaspoon parsley

Directions:

1. Cook the pasta and drain. Rinse with cool water and shake in a strainer until excess water is removed. Pour into a large bowl.

2. Add olive oil and lemon juice, toss pasta to coat.

3. Add the chopped vegetables and combine. Sprinkle with herbs and pour the can of tomatoes on the top, juices included.

4. Allow the salad to chill in the refrigerator for at least one hour. Serve alone or on top of large lettuce leaves.

Nutritional Information (Per Serving)

Calories: 397

Fat: 7.4 g

Sat Fat: 1.1 g

Carbohydrates: 75 g

Fiber: 10.7 g

Sugar: 0.1 g

Protein: 10.9 g
Sodium: 31.1 mg

Avocado Salsa and Turkey Wraps

Yield: 4 servings
Ingredients:
6 ounces low sodium deli turkey, sliced
¼ cup avocado
2 tablespoons salsa
2 whole-wheat tortillas
1 cup green cabbage, shredded
½ cup carrots, thinly sliced
½ cup tomatoes, thinly sliced

Directions:
1. In a small bowl, mash the avocado and mix in the salsa.

2. Next, spread the avocado salsa on two tortillas.

3. Evenly split the cabbage, carrots, tomato, and turkey between the two tortillas and center the ingredients allowing them to run the length of the tortillas.

4. Fold closest side of tortilla up toward you. Next, fold the sides in and roll up the wrap so that the seam is on the bottom.

5. Cut each tortilla in half and serve.

Nutritional Information (Per Serving)
Calories: 205
Fat: 5.4 g
Sat Fat: 1.0 g
Carbohydrates: 25.5 g
Fiber: 3.5 g
Sugar: 1.5 g
Protein: 14.0 g
Sodium: 570 mg

Tantalizing Tuna Melt

Yield: 4 servings
Ingredients:
4 whole wheat flour tortillas
2 cans of chunk light tuna in water, drained
8 tomato slices
¼ cup red onion, chopped
¼ cup celery, chopped
2 tablespoons lemon juice
2 tablespoons extra virgin olive oil
4 tablespoons low-fat mozzarella cheese
Ground black pepper

Directions:
1, Empty the tuna out of the cans into a small bowl. Use a fork to mix it with the olive oil and lemon juice.

2. Add the celery and the onion. Sprinkle pepper into the mixture.

3. Preheat your oven to 325 degrees F.

4. Lay the tortillas on a cookie sheet and spoon the tuna mixture onto each one, dividing it evenly. Top each with two thick tomato slices and then cover with cheese.

5. Bake for about 10 minutes, until the cheese is melted.

6. Remove from oven and let cool for 2 minutes. Roll the tortilla into a wrap and enjoy.

Nutritional Information (Per Serving)
Calories: 269
Fat: 11.6 g
Sat Fat: 3.0 g
Carbohydrates: 21.7 g
Fiber: 1.9 g
Sugar: 0.2 g
Protein: 21.3 g
Sodium: 410 mg

Nutty Quinoa

Yield: 4 servings

Ingredients:

1 tablespoon extra-virgin olive oil

1 teaspoon curry powder

½ teaspoon ground cumin

1 cup quinoa, rinsed and drained

1 cup vegetable broth

1 cup water

¾ cup almonds, toasted

½ cup raisins

¾ cup fresh parsley, chopped

Directions:

1. In a medium pan, heat oil over medium-high heat. Add curry powder and cumin, and sauté for 1–2 minutes.

2. Add quinoa and sauté for 2 minutes.

3. Add vegetable broth and water, and stir to combine. Cover and reduce heat to low. Simmer for 20 minutes.

4. Remove from heat and set aside, covered for about 5 minutes.

5. Just before serving, add almonds and raisins, and toss to coat.

6. Drizzle with lemon juice and serve.

Nutritional Information (Per Serving)
Calories: 408
Fat: 19.8 g
Sat Fat: 1.6 g
Carbohydrates: 50.6 g
Fiber: 7.0 g
Sugar: 12.7 g
Protein: 12.4 g
Sodium: 254 mg

Rigatoni with Garlic and Broccoli

Yield: 2 servings

Ingredients:

1/3 pound rigatoni

2 cups broccoli tops

2 tablespoons Parmesan cheese

2 teaspoons olive oil

2 teaspoons minced garlic

Black pepper to taste

Directions:

1. Fill a large pot with water, bring to a boil then add rigatoni and cook until al dente. When cooked, drain thoroughly.

2. As the pasta is boiling, fill another pot with one inch of water and fit your steamer in the pot.

3. Add the broccoli and cover it then allow it to steam for 10 minutes or until tender.

4. Combine the broccoli and pasta in a large bowl and toss with garlic, olive oil, cheese, and black pepper.

5. Serve immediately.

Nutritional Information (Per Serving)

Calories: 356

Fat: 7.6 g

Sat Fat: 1.6 g

Carbohydrates: 61.4 g

Fiber: 5.3 g

Sugar: 1.4 g

Protein: 14.2 g

Sodium: 117 mg

Chicken Chili

Yield: 8 servings

Ingredients:

10 ounces skinless chicken, cooked

28 ounces canned crushed tomatoes, no salt added

2 cups black beans, no salt added

1 red onion, diced

2 stalks of celery, diced

1 red bell pepper, diced

2 jalapeno peppers, diced

2 cloves of garlic, minced

2 tablespoons red pepper flakes

1 tablespoon black pepper

1 tablespoon oregano

1 tablespoon olive oil

¼ cup water

Directions:

1. In a large soup pot, cook the celery, onion, peppers, and garlic in the olive oil for 5 minutes.

2. Add all remaining ingredients and cook, covered for 2 hours.

3. Stir occasionally while it simmers.

Nutritional Information (Per Serving)

Calories: 149

Fat: 3.4 g

Sat Fat: 0.6 g

Carbohydrates: 20.2 g

Fiber: 5.3 g

Sugar: 3.3 g

Protein: 13.1 g

Sodium: 402 mg

Chicken Kabobs

Yield: 10 servings

Ingredients:

3 tablespoons low-sodium soy sauce

2 tablespoons applesauce

3 tablespoons balsamic vinegar

2 tablespoons olive oil

3 tablespoons fresh ginger, chopped

3 tablespoons fresh garlic, chopped

1 teaspoon red pepper flakes, crushed

3 cups skinless, boneless chicken, cubed

2½ cups fresh pineapple cubes

2 red bell peppers, seeded and cubed

Directions:

1. In a large bowl, mix soy sauce, applesauce, vinegar, oil, ginger, garlic, and red pepper flakes.

2. Add the chicken and generously coat with marinade.

3. Cover and refrigerate for about 2-3 hours.

4. Preheat grill to medium-high heat. Grease grill grate.

5. Thread chicken, pineapple, and bell pepper onto skewers.

6. Grill for about 10-12 minutes or until desired doneness, flipping occasionally.

Nutritional Information (Per Serving)
Calories: 129
Fat: 4.3 g
Sat Fat: 0.8 g
Carbohydrates: 10 g
Fiber: 1.2 g
Sugar: 6 g
Protein: 13.3 g
Sodium: 293 mg

Stuffed Zucchini

Yield: 6 servings

Ingredients:

6 medium zucchinis, halved lengthwise
2 potatoes, peeled and cubed
4 teaspoons olive oil
2½ cups onion, chopped
1 serrano pepper, minced
2 garlic cloves, minced
1½ tablespoons fresh ginger, minced
2 tablespoons chickpea flour
1 teaspoon ground coriander
¼ teaspoon ground cumin
1½ cups frozen green peas, thawed
2 tablespoons fresh cilantro, chopped
½ teaspoon salt
Black pepper to taste

Directions:

1. Preheat the oven to 375 degrees F.

2. With a scooper, scoop out the pulp from zucchini halves, leaving about ¼" thick shell.

3. In a shallow roasting pan, arrange the zucchini halves, cut side up. Sprinkle the zucchini halves with a little salt.

4. In a pan of boiling water, cook the potatoes for about 2 minutes. Drain well and set aside.

5. In a nonstick skillet, heat oil over medium-high heat. Add onion, serrano pepper, garlic, and ginger, and sauté for 3 minutes.

6. Reduce heat to medium low. Stir in chickpea flour and spices, and cook for about 5 minutes. Stir in cooked potatoes, green peas, and cilantro, and remove from heat.

7. With a paper towel, pat dry the zucchini halves. Stuff the zucchini halves evenly with the veggie mixture.

8. Lightly grease a baking dish. Arrange the zucchini halves in the baking dish.

9. Bake, covered for about 20 minutes.

Nutritional Information (Per Serving)
Calories: 150
Fat: 3.4 g
Sat Fat: 0.5 g
Carbohydrates: 25.2 g
Fiber: 5.8 g
Sugar: 3.1 g
Protein: 5.0 g
Sodium: 240 mg

Chapter 4: DASH Diet Snack Recipes

Roasted Chickpeas

Yield: 4 servings

Ingredients:

1 (15-ounce) can low-sodium chickpeas, rinsed and drained

1 tablespoon extra-virgin olive oil

1 teaspoon dried marjoram, crushed

1 teaspoon ground cumin

½ teaspoon cayenne pepper

¼ teaspoon ground allspice

Directions:

1. Preheat oven to 450 degrees F. Arrange rack in upper third of the oven.

2. Pat chickpeas dry with paper towels. Add oil, marjoram, and spices and toss to coat.

3. Spread chickpeas onto rimmed baking sheet.

4. Bake for about 25-30 minutes, stirring once mid-way through.

5. Remove from oven and set aside to cool on baking sheet for about 15 minutes.

Nutritional Information (Per Serving)
Calories: 147
Fat: 6 g
Sat Fat: 0.9 g
Carbohydrates: 16.7 g
Fiber: 5.2 g
Sugar: 0.6 g
Protein: 7.1 g
Sodium: 0.2 mg

Deviled Eggs

Yield: 6 servings

Ingredients:

6 large eggs

1 medium avocado, peeled, pitted, and chopped

2 teaspoons fresh lime juice

Pinch of salt

1/8 teaspoon cayenne pepper

Directions:

1. In a pot of water, hard boil eggs, cooking for about 15-20 minutes.

2. Drain water and let eggs cool completely.

3. Peel eggs and slice in half vertically with sharp knife.

4. Scoop out yolks and transfer half of them to bowl.

5. Add avocado, lime juice, and salt and mash with fork until well combined.

5. Fill egg halves with avocado mixture.

6. Sprinkle with cayenne pepper and serve.

Nutritional Information (Per Serving)

Calories: 140

Fat: 11.5 g

Sat Fat: 2.9 g

Carbohydrates: 3.3 g

Fiber: 2.3 g

Sugar: 0.6 g

Protein: 6.9 g

Sodium: 99 mg

Tomato Bruschetta

Yield: 6 servings

Ingredients:

½ whole-grain baguette, cut into 6 (½-inch-thick) slices on the diagonal

3 tomatoes, chopped

½ cup fennel, chopped

2 garlic cloves, minced

1 tablespoon fresh parsley, chopped

1 tablespoon fresh basil, chopped

2 teaspoons balsamic vinegar

1 teaspoon olive oil

Freshly ground black pepper to taste

Directions:

1. Preheat the oven to broil. Arrange rack in top portion of oven.

2. Arrange bread slices on baking sheet in single layer.

3. Broil for about 2 minutes per side.

4. Meanwhile, in bowl, add remaining ingredients and toss to coat.

5. Divide tomato mixture evenly and place on each slice of toasted bread. Serve immediately.

Nutritional Information (Per Serving)
Calories: 94.5
Fat: 1.5 g
Sat Fat: 0.1 g
Carbohydrates: 18 g
Fiber: 2.5 g
Sugar: 1.0 g
Protein: 3.7 g
Sodium: 176 mg

Fruit Smoothie

Yield: 2 servings
Ingredients:
1 banana
½ cup strawberries
½ cup blackberries
½ cup blueberries
Juice of 1 lemon
2 cups raw baby spinach
1 teaspoon fresh mint
1 cup ice

Directions:
1. Put everything in a blender and purée. Serve immediately.

Nutritional Information (Per Serving)
Calories: 98.3
Fat: 0.5 g
Sat Fat: 0.1 g
Carbohydrates: 24.2 g
Fiber: 5.4 g
Sugar: 12.7 g
Protein: 2.2 g
Sodium: 36.4 mg

Orange Dream Smoothie

Yield: 2 servings

Ingredients:

1 cup plain vanilla frozen yogurt

¾ cup fat-free milk

¼ cup frozen orange juice concentrate

Directions:

1. Put all ingredients in a blender and blend until creamy and smooth. Serve immediately.

Nutritional Information (Per Serving)

Calories: 163

Fat: 2.0 g

Sat Fat: 1.3 g

Carbohydrates: 26.7 g

Fiber: 0 g

Sugar: 14.3 g

Protein: 9.5 g

Sodium: 124 mg

Apple Cookies

Yield: 7 servings
Ingredients:
1 cup instant oats
¾ cup whole wheat flour
1½ teaspoons baking powder
1 teaspoon ground cinnamon
¼ teaspoon ground ginger
Pinch of ground cloves
Pinch of salt
1 large egg
½ cup applesauce
2 tablespoons unsalted butter, melted
1 teaspoon vanilla extract
1 cup apple, peeled, cored, and finely chopped

Directions:
1. In a bowl, mix together oats, flour, baking powder, spices, and salt.
2. Add remaining ingredients to a second large bowl except for apple and beat until well combined.
3. Add flour mixture to egg mixture and mix until just combined.
4. Fold apple in gently.
5. Chill in refrigerator for about 30 minutes.
6. Preheat oven to 325 degrees F. Line a cookie sheet with parchment paper.
7. With tablespoon, place mixture onto prepared cookie sheet in a single layer.
8. Flatten each cookie slightly using hands.
9. Bake for about 13-15 minutes.
10. Remove from oven and keep on wire rack to cool in pan for about 10 minutes.
11. Carefully turn onto wire rack until completely cooled.

Nutritional Information (Per Serving)
Calories: 140
Fat: 4.7 g
Sat Fat: 2.4 g
Carbohydrates: 21.6 g
Fiber: 2.1 g
Sugar: 5.4 g
Protein: 3.3 g
Sodium: 60 mg

Fruity Nut Bars

Yield: 24 bars
Ingredients:
½ cup quinoa flour
½ cup oats
¼ cup flax meal
¼ cup wheat germ
¼ cup chopped almonds
¼ cup dried apricots
¼ cup dried figs
¼ cup honey
2 tablespoons cornstarch

Directions:
1. Preheat the oven to 300 degrees F.
2. In a large bowl, combine all ingredients and mix thoroughly.
3. Spread mixture in a half an inch-thick layer in a parchment-lined sheet pan and bake for 20 minutes.
4. Let cool and cut.

Nutritional Information (Per Bar)
Calories: 53.8
Fat: 1.3 g
Sat Fat: 0.1 g
Carbohydrates: 9.7 g
Fiber: 1.4 g
Sugar: 4.7 g
Protein: 1.4 g
Sodium: 1.4 mg

Chapter 5: DASH Diet Dinner Recipes

When the dinner bell rings, it's time to fill up on delicious comfort food that won't compromise your health goals. Whether you're setting a table for one or calling the entire family to the table, make sure you have something good to serve. These DASH diet dinner recipes aren't complicated or time consuming. Make a little extra if you want to have leftovers for lunch the next day.

Salmon Curry

Yield: 4 servings

Ingredients:

1 tablespoon olive oil

1 small onion, chopped

2 garlic cloves, minced

1 teaspoon fresh ginger, minced

1 large tomatoes, peeled and chopped

½ tablespoon curry powder

¼ cup water

1¼ cups fat-free plain Greek yogurt, whipped

1½ pounds skinless salmon fillets cut into 2-inch cubes

¼ cup fresh parsley, chopped

Directions:

1. In a large skillet, heat oil on medium heat.

2. Add onion, garlic, and ginger and sauté for about 3-4 minutes.

3. Add tomatoes and cook for about 2-3 minutes, crushing with back of spoon.

4. Add curry paste and sauté for about 2 minutes.

5. Add water and yogurt and bring to a gentle boil.

6. Stir in salmon and cook for about 5-6 minutes or until desired doneness.

7. Serve hot, garnished with parsley.

Nutritional Information (Per Serving)

Calories: 322

Fat: 14.5 g

Sat Fat: 2 g

Carbohydrates: 8 g

Fiber: 1.4 g

Sugar: 4.8 g

Protein: 41.4 g

Sodium: 117 mg

Balsamic Chicken and Beans

Yield: 4 servings

Ingredients:

4 skinless, boneless chicken breasts

¼ cup balsamic vinegar

2 garlic cloves, minced

2 shallots, sliced

3 tablespoons extra virgin olive oil

1 pound fresh green beans, trimmed

2 tablespoons red pepper flakes

Directions:

1. Combine 2 tablespoons of the olive oil with the balsamic vinegar, garlic, and shallots. Pour it over the chicken breasts and refrigerate overnight.

2. The next day, preheat the oven to 375 degrees F.

3. Take the chicken out of the marinade and arrange in a shallow baking pan. Discard the rest of the marinade.

3. Bake in the oven for 40 minutes.

4. While the chicken is cooking, bring a large pot of water to a boil. Place the green beans in the water and allow them to cook for five minutes and then drain.

5. Heat one tablespoon of olive oil in the pot and return the green beans after rinsing them. Toss with red pepper flakes.

Nutritional Information (Per Serving)

Calories: 433

Fat: 17.4 g

Sat Fat: 3.3 g

Carbohydrates: 12.9 g

Fiber: 4.6 g

Sugar: 3.1 g

Protein: 56.1 g

Sodium: 140 mg

Vegetarian Chili

Yield: 8 servings

Ingredients:

2 cups onion, diced

1 cup celery, diced

1 cup bell pepper, diced

2 cloves garlic, minced

2 tablespoons water

2 jalapeño peppers, diced

4 cups crushed tomatoes, no salt added

2 cups canned pinto beans, drained and rinsed, no salt added

2 tablespoons cumin

1 tablespoon chipotle pepper

1 tablespoon black pepper

1 tablespoon balsamic vinegar

1 tablespoon oregano

Directions:

1. Add onion, celery, bell pepper, and garlic in 2 tablespoons of water in a stockpot over low heat. Cook until onions are translucent.

2. Add the rest of the ingredients. Cover and simmer for 1-2 hours, occasionally stirring.

3. If chili becomes too thick, thin it with water, adding small increments of water at a time.

Nutritional Information (Per Serving)

Calories: 115

Fat: 1.2 g

Sat Fat: 0.2 g

Carbohydrates: 22.9 g

Fiber: 6.7 g

Sugar: 0.8 g

Protein: 5.6 g

Sodium: 27.1 mg

Chickpeas and Barley Soup

Yield: 8 servings

Ingredients:

1 cup dry barley

1 (15-ounce) can low-sodium chickpeas, rinsed and drained

2 large carrots, peeled and chopped

1 zucchini, chopped

2 celery stalks, chopped

1 onion, chopped

2 cups tomatoes, chopped

1 teaspoon dried parsley, crushed

1 teaspoon curry powder

1 teaspoon paprika

3 bay leaves

Freshly ground black pepper to taste

5 cups low-sodium vegetable broth

4 cups water

½ cup fresh cilantro, chopped

Directions:

1. In large soup pan, add all ingredients except for parsley and bring to a boil on high heat.

2. Reduce heat to medium-low. Cover and simmer for about 1½ hours.

3. Discard bay leaf before serving.

4. Serve hot, garnishing with cilantro.

Nutritional Information (Per Serving)

Calories: 312

Fat: 4 g

Sat Fat: 0.5 g

Carbohydrates: 55.9 g

Fiber: 15.1 g

Sugar: 9.1 g

Protein: 15.5 g
Sodium: 85 mg

Vegetable Stew

Yield: 5 servings

Ingredients:

2 tablespoons olive oil

1 large onion, chopped

2 garlic cloves, minced

¼ teaspoon fresh ginger, finely grated

1 teaspoon ground cumin

1 teaspoon cayenne pepper

Freshly ground black pepper to taste

2 cups low-sodium vegetable broth

1½ cups small broccoli florets

1 cup cabbage, shredded

2 large carrots, peeled and sliced

1 teaspoon fresh lemon zest, finely grated

Directions:

1. In a large soup pan, heat oil on medium heat.

2. Add onion and sauté for about 3-4 minutes.

3. Add garlic, turmeric, ginger, and spices and sauté for about 1 minute.

4. Add 1 cup of broth and bring to a boil.

5. Add vegetables and bring to boil once more.

6. Cover and simmer for about 15-20 minutes, stirring occasionally.

7. Serve hot, topped with lemon zest.

Nutritional Information (Per Serving)

Calories: 96

Fat: 5.9 g

Sat Fat: 0.8 g

Carbohydrates: 9.6 g

Fiber: 2.6 g

Sugar: 3.7 g

Protein: 2.5 g

Sodium: 62 mg

Lentil and Spinach Chili

Yield: 8 servings

Ingredients:

2 teaspoons olive oil

1 large onion, chopped

3 medium carrot, peeled and chopped

4 celery stalks, chopped

2 garlic cloves, minced

1 jalapeño pepper, seeded and chopped

½ tablespoon dried thyme, crushed

1 tablespoon chipotle chili powder

½ tablespoon cayenne pepper

1½ tablespoons ground coriander

1½ tablespoons ground cumin

1 teaspoon ground turmeric

Freshly ground black pepper to taste

2 tablespoons tomato paste

1 pound lentils, rinsed

8 cups low-sodium vegetable broth

6 cups fresh spinach

½ cup fresh cilantro, chopped

½ cup sour cream

Directions:

1. In a large pan, heat oil on medium.

2. Add onion, carrot, and celery and sauté for about 5 minutes.

3. Add garlic, jalapeño pepper, thyme, and spices and sauté for about 1 minute.

4. Add tomato paste, lentils, and broth and bring to a boil.

5. Reduce heat to low and simmer for about 2 hours.

6. Stir in spinach and simmer for about 3-4 minutes.

7. Stir in cilantro and remove from heat.

8. Serve hot, topped with sour cream.

Nutritional Information (Per Serving)
Calories: 309
Fat: 6.1 g
Sat Fat: 2.3 g
Carbohydrates: 44.8 g
Fiber: 20.1 g
Sugar: 4.1 g
Protein: 19.4 g
Sodium: 144 mg

Stuffed Chicken Breast

Yield: 4 servings

Ingredients:

4 (4-ounce) skinless, boneless chicken breast halves, pounded to ½-inch thickness

Pinch of salt

Freshly ground black pepper to taste

¼ cup Kalamata olives, pitted and chopped

¼ cup oil packed sun-dried tomatoes, drained

¼ cup feta cheese, crumbled

1 tablespoon fresh dill, chopped

1 tablespoon fresh parsley, chopped

1 tablespoon olive oil

Directions:

1. Preheat oven to 375 degrees F. Grease a rimmed baking sheet.

2. Rub chicken with pinch of salt and black pepper.

3. In a large bowl, mix olives, tomatoes, feta cheese, scallion, dill, and parsley.

4. Place chicken breast on cutting board.

5. Stuff chicken breasts with olive mixture and roll tightly.

6. Secure each roll with toothpicks.

7. In a skillet, heat oil on medium-high heat.

8. Add chicken breast rolls and cook for about 2 minutes per side.

9. Arrange the chicken breast on prepared baking sheet in a single layer.

10. Bake for about 15-20 minutes or until desired doneness.

11. Remove from oven and set aside for about 5 minutes.

12. With a sharp knife, cut into slices and serve.

Nutritional Information (Per Serving)

Calories: 223
Fat: 11.5 g
Sat Fat: 3.7 g
Carbohydrates: 3 g
Fiber: 0.8 g
Sugar: 0.4 g
Protein: 27.3 g
Sodium: 278 mg

Turkey with Peas

Yield: 5 servings

Ingredients:

1 tablespoon olive oil

1 medium onion, chopped

½ teaspoon fresh ginger, minced

4 garlic cloves, minced

1½ teaspoons ground coriander

½ teaspoon ground cumin

½ teaspoon ground turmeric

¼ teaspoon ground nutmeg

2 bay leaves

1 pound lean ground turkey

½ cup fresh tomatoes, chopped

1-1½ cups water

1 cup fresh green peas, shelled

Pinch of salt

Freshly ground black pepper to taste

¼ cup fresh cilantro, chopped

Directions:

1. In a large pan, heat oil on medium-high heat.

2. Add onion and sauté for about 3-4 minutes.

3. Add ginger, garlic cloves, and spices and sauté for about 1 minute.

4. Add turkey and cook for about 5 minutes.

5. Add tomatoes and cook for about 10 minutes.

6. Stir in water and green peas. Cover and cook for about 25-30 minutes.

7. Stir in salt and black pepper. Remove from heat when desired doneness.

8. Serve hot, garnishing with cilantro.

Nutritional Information (Per Serving)

Calories: 196
Fat: 9.6 g
Sat Fat: 2.5 g
Carbohydrates: 8.2 g
Fiber: 2.4 g
Sugar: 3.1 g
Protein: 20 g
Sodium: 107 mg

Tilapia with Veggies

Yield: 2 servings
Ingredients:
2 (3-ounce) tilapia fillets
1 cup zucchini, sliced
1 cup summer squash, sliced
1 cup tomato, sliced
1 cup red bell pepper, seeded and sliced
1 cup red onion, sliced
2 tablespoons fresh rosemary, minced
Pinch of salt
Freshly ground black pepper to taste
3 teaspoons olive oil

Directions:
1. Preheat the oven to 350 degrees F. Grease a large baking dish.
2. Place all ingredients except for oil in large bowl and toss to coat.
3. Transfer mixture into prepared baking dish.
4. Bake for about 20-25 minutes.
5. Transfer mixture to serving plate.
6. Drizzle with oil and serve.

Nutritional Information (Per Serving)
Calories: 220
Fat: 8.9 g
Sat Fat: 1.7 g
Carbohydrates: 19.9 g
Fiber: 5.8 g
Sugar: 11 g
Protein: 19.3 g
Sodium: 152 mg

Rice and Lentil Casserole

Yield: 6 servings
Ingredients:
2½ cups water, divided
1 cup red lentils
½ cup wild rice
1 teaspoon olive oil
1 small onion, chopped
3 garlic cloves, minced
1/3 cup zucchini, chopped
1/3 cup carrot, peeled and chopped
1/3 cup celery stalk, chopped
1 fresh tomato, chopped
8-ounce low-sodium tomato sauce
1 teaspoon ground cumin
1 teaspoon dried oregano, crushed
1 teaspoon dried basil, crushed
Freshly ground black pepper to taste

Directions:
1. In a pan, add rice and 1 cup of water and bring to boil on medium heat.

2. Reduce heat to low, cover, and simmer for about 20 minutes.

3. Meanwhile, in another pan, add remaining water and lentils and bring to boil on medium heat.

4. Reduce heat to low, cover, and simmer, for about 15 minutes.

5. Transfer cooked rice and lentils to casserole dish and set aside.

6. Preheat oven to 350 degrees F.

7. In large skillet, heat oil on medium heat.

8. Add onion and garlic and sauté for about 4-5 minutes.

9. Add zucchini, carrots, celery, tomato, and tomato paste and cook for about 4-5 minutes.

10. Stir in cumin, herbs, salt, and black pepper and remove from heat.

11. Transfer vegetable mixture into casserole dish with rice and lentils and stir to combine.

12. Bake for about 30 minutes.

Nutritional Information (Per Serving)
Calories: 192
Fat: 1.5 g
Sat Fat: 0.2 g
Carbohydrates: 34.5 g
Fiber: 12 g
Sugar: 3.9 g
Protein: 11.3 g
Sodium: 225 mg

Spicy Lamb with Peas

Yield: 4 servings
Ingredients:
1 tablespoon coconut oil
3 dried red chilies
1 (2") cinnamon stick
3 green cardamom pods
1 medium red onion, chopped
½ teaspoon fresh ginger, minced
4 garlic cloves, minced
1½ teaspoons ground coriander
½ teaspoon garam masala
½ teaspoon ground cumin
½ teaspoon ground turmeric
2 bay leaves
1 pound lean ground lamb
½ cup Roma tomatoes, chopped
1½ cups water
1 cup frozen green peas
¼ cup fresh cilantro, chopped
¼ teaspoon salt
Black pepper to taste

Directions:
1. In a Dutch oven, melt coconut oil over medium-high heat. Add red chilies, cinnamon stick, and cardamom pods, and sauté for about 30 seconds.
2. Add onion and sauté for about 3–4 minutes. Add ginger, garlic cloves, and spices, and sauté for 30 seconds.
3. Add lamb and cook for 5 minutes.
4. Add tomatoes and cook for about 10 minutes.
5. Stir in water and green peas, and cook, covered for about 20 minutes.
6. Stir in cilantro, salt, and pepper, and remove from heat.

7. Serve hot.

Nutritional Information (Per Serving)
Calories: 417
Fat: 30.5 g
Sat Fat: 14.6 g
Carbohydrates: 12.9 g
Fiber: 5.4 g
Sugar: 2.2 g
Protein: 21.8 g
Sodium: 247 mg

Open Faced Turkey Burgers

Yield: 4 servings
Ingredients:
1 pound ground turkey breast
1/3 cup whole grain oats
4 slices whole grain wheat bread
4 slices low fat cheddar cheese
1 cup raw spinach leaves
1 tomato, sliced
¼ red onion, sliced into rings
Ground black pepper
¼ cup chopped yellow onion
¼ cup chopped red bell pepper
2 tablespoons light mayonnaise

Directions:
1. Put the red pepper and yellow onion in a food processor and pulse until very fine. Combine with the turkey breast and the whole oats.

2. Heat a grill or a grill pan. While the grill heats up, form the turkey mixture into 4 patties of equal size.

3. Grill on each side, until cooked and allow the cheese to melt before you remove from grill.

4. While they are cooking, toast the bread. Spread a light layer of mayonnaise on the bread and place one turkey patty on each slice.

5. Top with spinach, tomato, and red onion. Sprinkle with black pepper.

Nutritional Information (Per Serving)
Calories: 503
Fat: 27.3 g
Sat Fat: 10.0 g
Carbohydrates: 21.0 g

Fiber: 2.6 g
Sugar: 2.3 g
Protein: 42.1 g
Sodium: 474 mg

Stuffed Bell Peppers

Yield: 4 servings
Ingredients:
½ pound shiitake mushrooms
1 cup celery stalk
2 garlic cloves, peeled
½ cup walnuts, chopped
2 tablespoons olive oil
Pinch of salt
Freshly ground black pepper to taste
4 small red bell peppers, halved and seeded

Directions:
1. Preheat oven to 400 degrees F. Grease baking sheet.
2. Remove stem and seeds from bell peppers.
3. In food processor, add mushrooms, celery, garlic, walnuts, oil, salt, and pepper and pulse until finely chopped.
4. Stuff bell peppers with mushroom mixture.
5. Arrange bell peppers onto prepared baking sheet.
6. Bake for about 20-25 minutes.

Nutritional Information (Per Serving)
Calories: 232
Fat: 16.7 g
Sat Fat: 1.6 g
Carbohydrates: 19.6 g
Fiber: 4.3 g
Sugar: 8.6 g
Protein: 6.1 g
Sodium: 199 mg

Pepper Tilapia with Spinach

Yield: 4 servings

Ingredients:

4 tilapia filets, 8 ounces each

4 cups fresh spinach

1 red onion, sliced

3 garlic cloves, minced

2 tablespoons extra virgin olive oil

3 lemons

1 tablespoon ground black pepper

1 tablespoon ground white pepper

1 tablespoon crushed red pepper

Directions:

1. Preheat the oven to 350 degrees F.

2. Place the fish in a shallow baking dish and juice two of the lemons.

3. Cover the fish in the lemon juice and then sprinkle the three types of pepper over the fish.

4. Slice the remaining lemon and cover the fish. Bake in the oven for 20 minutes.

5. While the fish cooks, sauté the garlic and onion in the olive oil. Add the spinach.

6. Serve the fish on top of the spinach.

Nutritional Information (Per Serving)

Calories: 323

Fat: 11.5 g

Sat Fat: 2.1 g

Carbohydrates: 10.3 g

Fiber: 2.6 g

Sugar: 1.1 g

Protein: 50.0 g

Sodium: 145 mg

Salmon Salad

Yield: 4 servings
Ingredients:
4 salmon filets, 6 ounces each
2 tablespoons lemon juice
1 garlic clove, minced
8 lemon slices
2 tablespoons fresh Italian parsley
¼ teaspoon salt
ground black pepper
6 cups mixed lettuce greens
2 tomatoes, chopped
¼ cup toasted almonds, salt-free
¼ cup extra virgin olive oil

Directions:
1. Preheat the oven to 350 degrees F.

2. Cover the salmon with lemon juice, garlic, and lemon slices. Sprinkle with parsley, salt, and pepper and bake for 15 minutes.

3. Mix the salad with lettuce, tomatoes, almonds, and olive oil. Place the salmon on top.

Nutritional Information (Per Serving)
Calories: 424
Fat: 28 g
Sat Fat: 3.9 g
Carbohydrates: 7.4 g
Fiber: 2.3 g
Sugar: 1.2 g
Protein: 36.5 g
Sodium: 234 mg

Turkey with Lentils and Veggies

Yield: 6 servings

Ingredients:

3 tablespoons olive oil, divided

1 onion, chopped

1 tablespoon fresh ginger, minced

4 garlic cloves, minced

3 Roma tomatoes, seeded and chopped finely

3 celery stalks, chopped

1 large carrot, peeled and chopped

1 cup dried red lentils, rinsed, soaked for 30 minutes and drained

1 cup chicken broth

1 cup water

1½ teaspoons cumin seeds

½ teaspoon cayenne pepper

1 pound lean ground turkey

1 jalapeño pepper, seeded and chopped

2 scallions, chopped

¼ cup fresh cilantro, chopped

Directions:

1, In a Dutch oven, heat 1 tablespoon of oil over medium heat.

2. Add onion, ginger, and garlic, and sauté for 3 minutes.

3. Stir in tomatoes, celery, carrot, lentils, chicken broth, and water, and bring to a boil.

4. Reduce the heat to low. Simmer, covered for about 30 minutes.

5. In a skillet, heat remaining oil over medium heat. Add cumin seeds, and sauté for 30 seconds.

6. Add paprika and sauté for 30 seconds. Transfer the mixture into a small bowl, and set aside.

7. In the same skillet, add turkey and cook for 4–5 minutes.

8. Add jalapeño and scallion, and cook for 3–4 minutes. Add spiced oil mixture, and stir to combine well.

9. Transfer the turkey mixture in simmering lentils, and simmer for 10–15 minutes or until desired doneness.

Nutritional Information (Per Serving)
Calories: 245
Fat: 12.8 g
Sat Fat: 2.8 g
Carbohydrates: 15.2 g
Fiber: 4.8 g
Sugar: 1.0 g
Protein: 19.3 g
Sodium: 262 mg

Southwestern Roasted Corn Soup

Yield: 12 servings

Ingredients:

4 cups corn kernels

1½ tablespoons olive oil

3 cups onion, chopped

2 cups celery, chopped

2 cups carrots, chopped

2 teaspoons garlic, chopped

1/4 cup all-purpose flour

1 teaspoon cumin

4 cups vegetable broth

2 cups water

2 jalapeno peppers, minced

1½ cups half-and-half

1/8 teaspoon white pepper

1 tablespoon parsley, chopped

Directions:

1. Heat the oven to 500 degrees F.

2. Place corn kernels on a baking sheet and roast until caramelized, about 8 minutes.

3. In a large pot, heat oil over medium-high heat. Add all vegetables except the jalapeño and corn and stir constantly. Cook until vegetables are tender.

4. Reduce heat and stir in the corn, flour, and cumin and be sure to stir until the flour is evenly dispersed.

5. Add the vegetable broth and jalapenos and simmer 30 minutes.

6. Stir in half-and-half, salt, pepper, and parsley. Remove from heat and serve.

Nutritional Information (Per Serving)
Calories: 110

Fat: 1.8 g
Sat Fat: 0.4 g
Carbohydrates: 21.9 g
Fiber: 3.2 g
Sugar: 4.9 g
Protein: 3.6 g
Sodium: 399 mg

Pasta a la Bruschetta

Yield: 4 servings

Ingredients:

1 pound whole grain penne pasta

6 San Marzano tomatoes, chopped

4 cloves of garlic, chopped

1 red onion, chopped

¼ cup extra virgin olive oil

4 tablespoons parmesan cheese

Bunch of fresh basil

Directions:

1. Cook pasta in large pot of water.

2. In a pan, heat half the olive oil and sauté garlic, onion, and tomatoes.

3. Once the pasta has finished cooking, drain. Add it to the sauté pan and combine with vegetables. Add the remaining olive oil.

4. Serve with fat free parmesan cheese sprinkled over it as well as fresh basil.

Nutritional Information (Per Serving)

Calories: 597

Fat: 18.2 g

Sat Fat: 3.9 g

Carbohydrates: 96.1 g

Fiber: 6.6 g

Sugar: 2.0 g

Protein: 18.2 g

Sodium: 111 mg

Meatballs Curry

Yield: 6 servings
Ingredients:
For Meatballs:
1 pound lean ground turkey
2 eggs, beaten
3 tablespoons red onion, minced
¼ cup fresh basil leaves, chopped
¼ teaspoon fresh ginger, chopped finely
4 garlic cloves, chopped finely
1 jalapeño pepper, seeded and minced
1 tablespoon red curry paste
1 tablespoon fish sauce
2 tablespoons coconut oil
For Curry:
1 red onion, chopped
4 garlic cloves, minced
½ teaspoon fresh ginger, minced
1 jalapeño pepper, seeded and minced
1 tablespoon red curry paste
1 (14 oz.) can coconut milk
2 tablespoons fresh lime juice
Black pepper to taste

Directions:
1. For meatballs, in a large bowl, add all ingredients except oil, and mix until well combined. Make small balls from the mixture.
2. In a large skillet, melt coconut oil over medium heat. Add meatballs and cook for 3–5 minutes or until golden brown on all sides. Transfer the meatballs into a bowl.
3. In the same skillet, add onion, and sauté for 3 minutes.
4. Add garlic, ginger, and jalapeño, and sauté for 1 minute.
5. Add curry paste, and sauté for 1 minute.

6. Add coconut milk and meatballs, and bring to a gentle simmer. Reduce heat to low and simmer, covered for about 10 minutes.

7. Serve with a drizzling of lime juice.

Nutritional Information (Per Serving)
Calories: 346
Fat: 19.1 g
Sat Fat: 8.9 g
Carbohydrates: 22.8 g
Fiber: 1.5 g
Sugar: 5.2 g
Protein: 24.4 g
Sodium: 607 mg

Chicken Kebab

Yield: 4 servings
Ingredients:
12 ounces cooked chicken, cut into pieces
2 red bell peppers, chopped
1 red onion, chopped
2 cups cherry or grape tomatoes
1 cup button mushrooms
1 cup pineapple chunks
2 tablespoons olive oil
Ground black pepper

Directions:

1. Heat a grill or a grill pan and place the meat, vegetables, and pineapple chunks on skewers in any pattern that appeals to you.

2. Brush each kebab with olive oil and sprinkle with pepper.

3. Heat the kebabs on the grill, turning to ensure all sides are cooked.

4. Remove from the grill and serve with a side of salad or a bowl of fruit.

Nutritional Information (Per Serving)
Calories: 226
Fat: 9.6 g
Sat Fat: 1.6 g
Carbohydrates: 14.6 g
Fiber: 3.4 g
Sugar: 6.3 g
Protein: 21.3 g
Sodium: 52.1 mg

Chapter 6: DASH Diet Dessert Recipes

Frozen Fruity Treat

Yield: 6 servings
Ingredients:
14-ounce unsweetened almond milk
1 cup frozen pineapple chunks, thawed
4 cups frozen banana slices, thawed
2 tablespoons fresh lime juice
Pinch of salt

Directions:
1. Line glass baking dish with plastic wrap.
2. In high speed blender, add all ingredients and pulse until smooth.
3. Transfer mixture to prepared baking dish and spread evenly.
4. Freeze for about 35-40 minutes before serving.

Nutritional Information (Per Serving)
Calories: 135
Fat: 1.3 g
Sat Fat: 0.2 g
Carbohydrates: 32.5 g
Fiber: 3.3 g
Sugar: 20.9 g
Protein: 1.5 g
Sodium: 77 mg

Ricotta Mousse

Yield: 2 servings

Ingredients:

2½ cups water, divided

1 cup ricotta cheese

2 teaspoons stevia powder

2 teaspoons cocoa powder

½ teaspoon pure vanilla extract

2 tablespoons fresh blackberries

Directions:

1. In large bowl, add all ingredients except for blackberries and beat until well combined.

2. Transfer mousse into 2 serving glasses and refrigerate to chill for about 4-6 hours or until completely set.

3. Garnish with blackberries and serve.

Nutritional Information (Per Serving)

Calories: 182

Fat: 10.2 g

Sat Fat: 6.3 g

Carbohydrates: 8.2 g

Fiber: 1 g

Sugar: 1 g

Protein: 14.6 g

Sodium: 155 mg

Chickpea Fudge

Yield: 12 servings

Ingredients:

2 cups chickpeas, cooked

8 Medjool dates, pitted and chopped

½ cup almond butter

½ cup unsweetened almond milk

1 teaspoon vanilla extract

2 tablespoons cocoa powder

Directions:

1. Line a large baking dish with parchment paper.

2. In food processor, add all ingredients except for cocoa powder and pulse until well combined.

3. Transfer mixture to large bowl.

4. Stir in cocoa powder.

5. Divide mixture evenly and transfer to prepared baking dish. Smooth surface with a spatula.

6. Refrigerate for about 2 hours or until completely set.

7. Cut into desired sized squares and serve.

Nutritional Information (Per Serving)

Calories: 146

Fat: 2.7 g

Sat Fat: 0.4 g

Carbohydrates: 25 g

Fiber: 6.6 g

Sugar: 7.1 g

Protein: 6.9 g

Sodium: 16 mg

Grapefruit Yogurt Bowl

Yield: 2 servings
Ingredients:
½ grapefruit
1 cup strawberries, chopped
1 teaspoon brown sugar
1 cup fat-free vanilla yogurt
¼ cup walnuts
¼ cup blueberries

Directions:

1. Scoop out the grapefruit segments from the rind and place in a bowl.

2. Add the strawberries and blueberries and combine. Toss the fruit mixture with the brown sugar.

3. Place the yogurt in the hollow grapefruit shell. Spoon the fruit mixture onto the yogurt and sprinkle the top with walnuts.

Nutritional Information (Per Serving)
Calories: 224
Fat: 10.6 g
Sat Fat: 1.0 g
Carbohydrates: 26 g
Fiber: 3.9 g
Sugar: 21.9 g
Protein: 10.2 g
Sodium: 97.1 mg

Apple Crisp

Yield: 4 servings

Ingredients:

For Filling:

2 large Granny Smith apples, peeled, cored, and chopped

2 tablespoons water

2 tablespoons fresh apple juice

¼ teaspoon ground cinnamon

For Topping:

½ cup quick rolled oats

¼ cup unsweetened coconut flakes

2 tablespoons pecans, chopped

½ teaspoon ground cinnamon

¼ cup water

Directions:

1. Preheat oven to 300 degrees F. Lightly grease baking dish.

2. In large mixing bowl, place all filling ingredients and mix gently.

3. Transfer mixture to prepared baking dish.

4. In another bowl, mix together all topping ingredients.

5. Evenly spread topping over filling mixture.

6. Bake for about 20 minutes or until topping is golden brown.

Nutritional Information (Per Serving)

Calories: 194

Fat: 4.1 g

Sat Fat: 1.6 g

Carbohydrates: 39.5 g

Fiber: 23.8 g

Sugar: 2.5 g

Protein: 6.9 g

Sodium: 9 mg

Fruit and Nut Parfait

Yield: 4 servings
Ingredients:
1 cup melon
1 banana
1 cup mixed berries
¼ cup raisins
½ cup walnuts
2 cups fat free vanilla yogurt

Directions:
1. Cut the melon into chunks that are about the same size as your berries and slice the banana. Mix in a large bowl with the raisins and the walnuts.

2. Top with the yogurt and blend to combine.

3. Chill for about 30 minutes and serve in two separate bowls.

Nutritional Information (Per Serving)
Calories: 253
Fat: 10.5 g
Sat Fat: 1.1 g
Carbohydrates: 33.7 g
Fiber: 3.7 g
Sugar: 24.9 g
Protein: 10.4 g
Sodium: 104 mg

Final Thoughts

Finally, I want to thank you for reading my book. If you enjoyed the book, please take the time to share your thoughts and post a review on the <u>DASH Diet for Beginners: Easy and Delicious DASH Diet Recipes to Lose Weight and Lower Blood Pressure</u> Amazon book page. It would be greatly appreciated!

Best wishes,
Savannah Gibbs

Check Out My Other Books

Mediterranean Diet Cookbook: Easy and Delicious
Mediterranean Diet Recipes to Lose Weight and Lower Your
Risk of Heart Disease
https://www.amazon.com/dp/B071RMNKJG/

Clean Eating Cookbook: Quick and Easy Clean Eating Recipes
to Lose Weight and Live Healthy
https://www.amazon.com/dp/B06XX7R39Y/

Weight Loss Smoothies: 45 Delicious Smoothie Recipes to
Lose Weight and Get Healthy
https://www.amazon.com/Weight-Loss-Smoothies-Delicious-
Smoothie-ebook/dp/B06XHF9RXM/

Paleo Diet Cookbook: Easy and Delicious Paleo Recipes to
Lose Weight and Get Healthy
https://www.amazon.com/Paleo-Diet-Cookbook-Delicious-
Recipes-ebook/dp/B06XK9JG4D/

Slow Cooker Cookbook: Easy, Delicious, and Healthy Slow
Cooker Recipes for Your Family
https://www.amazon.com/dp/B06XCGQFP3/

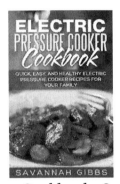

Electric Pressure Cooker Cookbook: Quick, Easy, and Healthy
Electric Pressure Cooker Recipes for Your Family
https://www.amazon.com/Electric-Pressure-Cooker-
Cookbook-Healthy-ebook/dp/B06XD7RRHZ/

Essential Oils for Beginners: 56 Best Essential Oil Recipes for
Your Health and Beauty
https://www.amazon.com/dp/B01MXYTEW7/

72204595R00066

Made in the USA
San Bernardino, CA
22 March 2018